D1455976

Leaving a Light Footprint

Andrew Einspruch

This edition first published in 2011 in the United States of America by Smart Apple Media. All rights reserved. No part of this book may be reproduced in any form or by any means without written permission from the publisher.

Smart Apple Media
P.O. Box 3263
Mankato, MN, 56002

First published in 2010 by
MACMILLAN EDUCATION AUSTRALIA PTY LTD
15–19 Claremont St, South Yarra, Australia 3141

Visit our web site at www.macmillan.com.au or go directly to www.macmillanlibrary.com.au

Associated companies and representatives throughout the world.

Copyright © Andrew Einspruch 2010

Library of Congress Cataloging-in-Publication Data

Einspruch, Andrew.
    Leaving a light footprint / Andrew Einspruch.
       p. cm. — (Living sustainably)
    Includes index.
    ISBN 978-1-59920-556-4 (library binding)
    1. Environmental responsibility—Juvenile literature. 2. Nature—Effect of human beings on—Juvenile literature.
    3. Sustainable living—Juvenile literature. I. Title.
    GE195.7.E46 2011
    304.2—dc22
                        2009045102

Publisher: Carmel Heron
Managing Editor: Vanessa Lanaway
Editor: Laura Jeanne Gobal
Proofreader: Helena Newton

Designer: Kerri Wilson (cover and text)
Page layout: Kerri Wilson
Photo Researcher: Jes Senbergs (management: Debbie Gallagher)
Production Controller: Vanessa Johnson

Manufactured in China by Macmillan Production (Asia) Ltd.
Kwun Tong, Kowloon, Hong Kong
Supplier Code: CP January 2010

Acknowledgments
The author and the publisher are grateful to the following for permission to reproduce copyright material:

Front cover photograph of a family hiking on a wooded path, courtesy of © Soundsnaps/iStockphoto.

Photographs courtesy of Rob Cruse, **20**; Dugald Bremner/Getty Images, **8**; Harald Eisenberger/Getty Images, **9**; Jamie Grill/Getty Images, **12**; Jupiterimages/Getty Images, **30**; Jonathan Knowles/Getty Images, **29**; Geri Lavrov/Getty Images, **23**; Philippe Marchand/Getty Images, **11**; Ben Osbourne/Getty Images, **3**, **16**; Paul Viant/Getty Images, **5**; Peter Ziminski/Getty Images, **4**; © Andrew Howe/iStockphoto, **19**; Jupiter Images, **13**; Newspix/News Ltd/Julie Best, **26**; Newspix/News Ltd/Peter Clark, **27**; Photolibrary © Nick Hanna/Alamy, **10**; Photolibrary © Photas Ltd/Alamy, **7**; Photolibrary © Paula Solloway/Alamy, **24**; Photolibrary © Vespasian/Alamy, **28**; Photolibrary © Richard Wayman/Alamy, **21**; Photolibrary/Peter Bennett, **25**; Photolibrary/Lester Lefkowitz, **18**; Photolibrary/Graham Monro, **15**; Photolibrary/Juan Carlos Munoz, **14**; Photolibrary/Patti Murray, **17**; Picture Media/Reuters/Reinhard Krause, **6**; Zero Waste SA, **22**.

While every care has been taken to trace and acknowledge copyright, the publisher tenders their apologies for any accidental infringement where copyright has proved untraceable. Where the attempt has been unsuccessful, the publisher welcomes information that would redress the situation.

Contents

When a word is printed in **bold**, you can look up its meaning in the Glossary on page 31.

Living Sustainably

Living sustainably means using things carefully so there is enough left for people in the future. To live sustainably, we need to look after Earth and its **resources**.

If we cut down too many trees now, there will not be enough lumber in the future.

The things we do make a difference. We can use water, energy, and other resources wisely. Our choices can help make a sustainable world.

Reducing waste by **recycling** is one way of using Earth's resources wisely.

Leaving a Light Footprint

Almost everything we do affects Earth. When we switch on a light or buy a new toy, we use Earth's resources. Our actions can sometimes harm Earth.

When we travel in a car powered by gasoline, we are using Earth's resources.

We all make choices about how we live. Choosing to live sustainably means making choices that affect Earth as little as possible. This is called leaving a light footprint.

Drying the washing in the sun uses fewer resources than a dryer, which uses electricity.

Do Not Disturb

Campers have a saying: "Take only pictures, leave only footprints." It means when we enjoy the outdoors, we should leave the area as we found it.

To protect Earth, we must not change or damage its natural environment.

Whenever we make a choice, we should ask ourselves, "Will this choice leave only footprints?" Choices that leave only footprints are sustainable ones.

Bicycles do not use gasoline, which means they leave a lighter footprint than cars.

Growing Food

Growing our own vegetables is one way to leave a light footprint. Homegrown food uses fewer resources than food that has come from somewhere else.

Everyone can try to grow some vegetables at home, even people who live in apartments.

Extra fruit can be made into jam and stored.

When we grow food, we often end up with extra. Freezing and drying the extras are good ways of storing food for later use.

Being Responsible Outdoors

The outdoors can be fun, but we need to be responsible when enjoying it. The most important rule is, "Do not litter." We should always take garbage away with us.

Collecting our garbage protects the environment and animals from the harm that littering causes.

Avoid disturbing any animals, including insects, and do not bring any plants home. Plants should be left to grow in their natural environment.

Leave plants and animals alone so that people in the future can enjoy them, too.

Protecting Biodiversity

Biodiversity is the variety of plants and animals in a certain environment. Biodiversity is important to the health of every environment on Earth.

Rain forests are the most biodiverse environments because they have many different types of plants and animals.

Plants and animals that belong to a certain environment depend on each other to survive. When this environment is not treated carefully, plants and animals may die.

Some parks allow only leashed dogs in so that other animals are not harmed.

Threats to Biodiversity

Our actions can threaten biodiversity. Hunting, pollution, and **logging** are examples of actions that threaten biodiversity.

Oil spills are a type of pollution that is harmful to biodiversity.

Many other actions affect biodiversity, too. Litter, for example, can make its way into an animal's **habitat**. Animals might eat the litter and choke on it.

Plastic litter can be very dangerous to birds, who might choke on it.

Using Energy Wisely

To leave a light footprint, we must use energy wisely. Most energy comes from **fossil fuels** such as coal and oil. Burning these fuels adds to pollution and **global warming**.

When coal is burned to release energy, it also releases smoke, which pollutes the air.

Fossil fuels are also nonrenewable. This means once they are used up, they cannot be replaced.

Cars run on gasoline, which comes from oil, a nonrenewable resource.

How Can We Use Energy Wisely?

We can save energy at home by:
- turning televisions and computers off at the wall plug or unplugging them
- taking shorter showers to use less hot water
- switching lights off when leaving a room

Turning the computer off at the wall plug or unplugging it is an easy way to save energy.

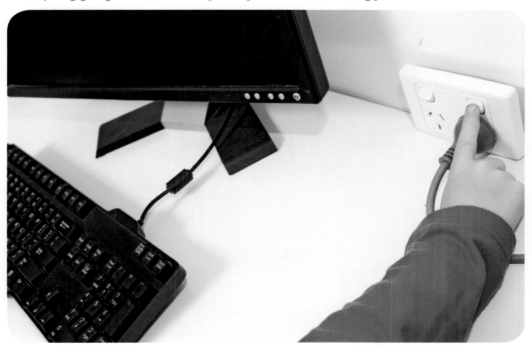

We can save energy at school by:
- using natural sunlight to brighten the classroom
- opening windows and doors on hot days to let a cool breeze in
- sharing a car ride to school with friends so fewer cars are used

Using natural sunlight instead of electric lights helps schools cut down on their energy use.

Working Toward Zero Waste

Zero waste means there is no waste. Zero waste is a goal of some communities. They try to recycle or **compost** their waste instead of throwing it into a garbage tip.

At this waste center, workers sort waste for different kinds of recycling.

We can help achieve zero waste by:
- buying things that can be recycled
- making things instead of buying them when possible
- not buying products with a lot of **packaging**

When something is recycled, it can be used again and does not become waste.

Get Involved in Your Community

It is easier to practice living sustainably when everyone in a community works together. Many towns and cities have started projects that help people practice sustainable living.

Community gardens give us the opportunity to grow our own vegetables and leave a lighter footprint.

We can get involved in our community by:
- taking part in clean-up days
- helping out with tree-planting projects
- joining a local **conservation** group

Removing litter from a beach helps keep the
sea clean and wildlife safe.

Make Changes at School

Schools can also leave a light footprint on Earth. Schools can do this by taking steps to save resources such as water and energy.

This school practices composting to reduce the amount of garden and food waste it creates.

Schools can leave a light footprint by:

- planting flowers, trees, and shrubs that do not need much water
- putting **mulch** on garden beds to save water
- using recycling bins to collect items that can be recycled

Many plants that grow naturally in an area need much less water than other plants.

Share the Message

Leaving a light footprint is an important message to share with your friends. Ask your teacher if your class can make posters to put up around the school.

These students are sharing the message by decorating rainwater tanks for their school.

A School Leaving a Light Footprint

Oak Hills Elementary School in California has a zero-waste program. Students use reusable containers and napkins. They also avoid eating packaged food.

Aim for zero waste at lunchtime by not eating packaged food.

A Sustainable World

Leaving a light footprint is one way to live sustainably. What can you do to have less of an impact on Earth? Your choices and actions will help make a sustainable world.

Make a list of the things you can do every day to leave a light footprint.

Glossary

compost decomposed natural material, usually made from kitchen scraps and garden waste

conservation activities aimed at taking care of Earth and its natural environments

environment the air, water, and land that surround us

fossil fuels the buried remains of plants and animals that form fuels such as oil, coal, and natural gas after millions of years

global warming the rise of temperatures on Earth caused by polluting gases

habitat the natural environment of a plant or animal

logging cutting down trees for wood

mulch loose materials, such as woodchips or straw, spread over the ground to hold in moisture

packaging the material in which things are wrapped before they are sold

pollution waste that damages the air, water, or land

recycling creating something new out of something that has been used

resources useful things found on Earth that are hard to replace once they run out

Index